NOTE
TO SELF
JOURNAL

REBEKAH BALLAGH

NOTE TO SELF
JOURNAL

TOOLS TO TRANSFORM YOUR WORLD

How to create calm, confidence and clarity in your life

ALLEN&UNWIN
SYDNEY • MELBOURNE • AUCKLAND • LONDON

WELCOME!

It's so great you're here, and I hope you are proud of yourself for investing in your wellbeing with this interactive journal.

The pages to come are jam-packed with inspirational affirmations, thought-provoking journal prompts and exercises that will change your life. These transformative tools have come straight from the therapy room and landed here in the pages of this book.

I have hand-picked each of the exercises ahead as some of the most powerful and effective instruments of change that I have discovered in my years of counselling work and in my own journey with anxiety, self-doubt and tough times.

If you have ever struggled with worries and anxiety, times of depression or general mood slumps, feelings of low self-worth or a lack of confidence, then you are in the right place. This journal is also perfect if your goal is to further cement the hard work you have already put into yourself, by adding some tools to support your continuing journey to wellness.

Remember that change takes practice and it takes work. Trying a tool or doing an exercise just once may be lovely, it may even spark some 'aha!' moments, but in order to create big shifts and lasting changes, try to turn these practices into habits by repeating them, over and over again.

When you do this, you create new neural pathways in your brain; and the more you repeat a new healthy behaviour, the more you cement and strengthen these pathways. Doing this helps to override existing unhelpful or unhealthy habits and responses.

Remember these old habits and ways of thinking may have been around a while. You may have spent years practising how to be anxious, how to get stuck in a slump and how to judge yourself harshly! So try not to beat yourself up if it takes a bit of practice to get out of these old ways. It's normal to struggle and to get stuck at times. It's also normal to fall back into old ways; they are, after all, our 'default', so they're easy and familiar to us. Just know that it's worth the effort to continue to push through and make change. The tools here truly do hold the power to completely change your life.

How to use this journal

Exercises, affirmations and journal prompts are dispersed throughout this book in no particular order so you can dip in and out as you like with no pressure to use them in a specific way. There are breathing exercises, grounding practices, mindfulness tools, brain dumps, check-ins, body scans, visualisations and more.

You'll likely want to return to many of these tools and do them again and again, so you may like to photocopy some of the logs and prompts to re-use as often as you need.

REBEKAH BALLAGH

> Let's get things started with a coffee . . .

HOT COFFEE BREATH

STEP 1

Imagine that you are holding a cup of hot coffee in your hands (you can try this while visualising other things too — a cup of tea, soup, your favorite winter stew or a hot chocolate).

STEP 2

As you slowly inhale through your nose, imagine you are breathing in the rich aroma of your coffee.

STEP 3

Slowly exhale through pursed lips, as though you were trying to cool down the hot coffee before taking a sip.

STEP 4

Repeat steps 1-3 for a few minutes (or as long as you like). You may even notice a gentle warming feeling in your hands as this lovely breathing technique soothes and relaxes you.

What are some of the unhelpful beliefs I have about myself?
What are some examples from my life that prove these aren't true?

_____

_____

_____

_____

_____

_____

_____

_____

_____

_____

_____

_____

_____

_____

_____

_____

_____

_____

SQUARE BREATHING

Try out this simple breathing technique as you slow down and regulate your nervous system.

Square breathing helps improve your focus and relax your body. You may find the counting and rhythm helpful in focusing your racing mind. The idea here is to even out your inhale and exhale and deepen your breath. You can breathe in and out through your nose, or you may find that exhaling through your mouth helps to slow your breath down in a more even way.

You may like to trace your finger around the square on this page as you count — begin by exhaling all the air out of your lungs, then start your count of 4 seconds on your next inhale.

BREATHING RATE RECORD

It's time to get a gauge of **your** breathing rate. This simple exercise will provide you with some super useful feedback: by assessing if you are 'over-breathing' you can get a good gauge to indicate whether or not your body is in a 'stress response'.

First, let's find out how many breaths you take per minute.

HOW TO

STEP 1

Set a timer on your phone or keep an eye on your watch. You can either time yourself for a full minute, or for 30 seconds and then times this number by 2.

STEP 2

Start the timer and begin counting your breaths. 1 breath = a breath in **and** a breath out.

STEP 3

When your timer goes off and the minute is up, write your number of breaths here:

'_____ breaths per minute'

NOTE: Try not to alter or change the way you are breathing because you are counting and observing your breath! Also, make sure you don't do this right after you've climbed a flight of stairs and are feeling puffed, as this will alter your natural breathing rate.

Did you know . . . A 'normal' breathing rate for an adult who isn't under stress is between 12 and 20 breaths per minute.

If your breathing rate is faster that 20 breaths per minute you are 'overbreathing'.

Overbreathing creates an imbalance of CO_2 and O_2 in your body . . . You actually end up with **less** CO_2 than you need, and this can cause your brain to get 'over-excited' and to overthink . . . Overbreathing also creates these symptoms:

* feeling faint or lightheaded
* feeling anxious or panicky
* dizziness or tingling
* tight chest or pain in the chest

* frequent yawning or sighing
* faster heartbeart
* insomnia.

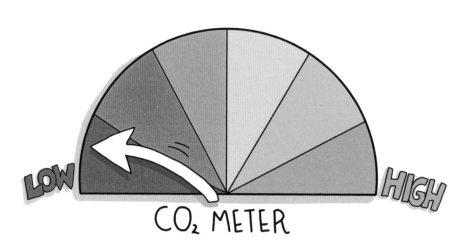

LOW   HIGH

CO₂ METER

What parts of myself do I judge myself on?
What can I do to begin to let go of this judgement?

_____
_____
_____
_____
_____
_____
_____
_____
_____
_____
_____
_____
_____
_____
_____
_____
_____
_____

Now that you have spent several minutes slowing your breathing, let's head back up to step 1 and take your breathing rate again — go ahead and do this now.

Write your new breathing rate here:

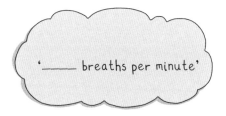

'_____ breaths per minute'

Did you notice that your new resting breathing rate has reduced from your original number? Slow breathing activates your parasympathetic nervous system, which calms you down and turns off your threat response.

If you noticed that you have a high breathing rate (over 20 breaths per minute) or that your breathing speeds up when you are anxious or stressed, try out the breathing-rate tracker on page 16 over the next week.

In this tracker, you will take your breathing rate before and after a calming breathing exercise, 3 times per day for 7 days. The hope is that over the course of the week you notice your 'before rate/resting breathing rate' and anxiety symptoms decreasing.

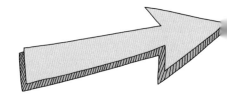

HOW TO USE THIS TRACKER

STEP 1

Take your 'before' or 'resting breathing rate' and write it into the log opposite.

STEP 2

Do 3 to 5 minutes of the calming breathing technique.

STEP 3

Take your 'after' breathing rate and write it into the log opposite.

STEP 4

Repeat steps 1-3 twice more each day and write your results in the log. You can pick 3 times throughout the day and write them in the 'time' space opposite; for example, you might pick 8am, 12pm and 7pm.

	Time _____		Time _____		Time _____	
	Before rate	After rate	Before rate	After rate	Before rate	After rate
Day 1						
Day 2						
Day 3						
Day 4						
Day 5						
Day 6						
Day 7						

You might like to take note of how you are feeling before and after you do your breathing exercise and whether you are experiencing any improvements in your symptoms of overbreathing.

Notes:
(e.g. anxiety, stress, triggers, your thoughts or observations, the situations you were in)

I WAS DOING
THE BEST I
COULD AT THE
TIME WITH WHAT
I KNEW

What areas of myself do I feel are unworthy of love?
How can I begin to accept these parts of myself?

_____

_____

_____

_____

_____

_____

_____

_____

_____

_____

_____

_____

_____

_____

_____

5 4 3 2 1 GROUNDING TOOL

Grounding is all about becoming present by tuning into your senses. Sit somewhere cosy, take a deep breath, become present in the room and notice . . .

5 things you can see

✻ _____
✻ _____
✻ _____
✻ _____
✻ _____

4 things you can hear

✻ _____
✻ _____
✻ _____
✻ _____

3 things you can feel

✻ _____
✻ _____
✻ _____

2 things you can smell

✻ _____
✻ _____

1 thing you can taste

✻ _____

MY SELF-
WORTH
IS NOT
DETERMINED
BY WHAT
OTHER
PEOPLE THINK
OF ME

List one thing about each part of your
body that you are grateful for . . .

_____

_____

_____

_____

_____

_____

_____

_____

_____

_____

_____

_____

_____

_____

_____

Take a well-deserved break with this lovely little mindful moment.

MINDFUL TEA DRINKING

Mindfulness is all about being non-judgementally aware of your experience in the current moment — intentionally shifting out of 'autopilot' and away from past-dwelling and future-ruminating into being present in the here and now. One of the simplest ways to practise mindfulness is to tune into your senses.

I'm sure none of us are strangers to boiling the kettle for a brew a few times a day, so next time you're reaching for the coffee mug, give this little grounding exercise a try.

STEP 1

Sit down somewhere cosy with your cup of tea.

STEP 2

Look around the room and notice the little details, perhaps taking note of some small features you don't often pay attention to or haven't seen before.

STEP 3

Close your eyes and make a list in your mind of all the things you can hear.

STEP 4

Direct your attention to your body. Notice the feeling of your back against your seat, perhaps your feet on the floor, the feeling of the hot mug in your hands ... Become aware of your physical experience in this moment.

STEP 5

Take a long, slow inhale of your cup of tea and savour the aroma.

STEP 6

Finally, take a sip of your cuppa, notice the heat on your tongue and the way it feels as you swallow. Pay attention to and describe the taste to yourself.

You may like to cycle back through each step as you drink your tea, staying grounded in the moment by focusing on your senses and your breath.

How often do you catch yourself comparing yourself to others?
How do you know you are doing it? How do you feel when you
compare yourself to others?

_____

_____

_____

_____

_____

_____

_____

_____

_____

_____

_____

_____

_____

_____

_____

_____

_____

What from your past are you 'caught up on'/ruminating about?
What do you need/need to hear/need to do in order to shift
away from this?

_____

_____

_____

_____

_____

_____

_____

_____

_____

_____

_____

_____

_____

_____

_____

_____

_____

SAFE PLACE VISUALISATION

Creating a safe or happy place is a visualisation tool that you can use whenever you need a calming escape. It's fantastic as a way of managing anxiety, stress, low mood, or even times when you are feeling triggered. Take your time creating a safe space that is just right for **you**.

Close your eyes and imagine a place where you feel safe. It could be somewhere imaginary. You might like to be at a beach, in a meadow, by a lake or stream, in a cosy library corner or a sunny study on a comfy chair.

Imagine the specifics:

❋ What do you smell?

❋ What do you see?

❋ What do you hear?

❋ What can you reach out and touch?

Drink it all in, imagining and creating more and more details. Breathe deep, slow breaths into your belly.

You can return here anytime you need to feel safe and at peace. Just close your eyes and breathe.

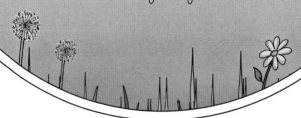

What parts of myself do I love and accept?

_____
_____
_____
_____
_____
_____
_____
_____
_____
_____
_____
_____
_____
_____
_____
_____
_____
_____
_____
_____

MINDFUL BODY SCAN

Slowly scan through each of the areas listed below, gently shifting your attention from one part of your body to the next, without judgement.

FOREHEAD

JAW

CHEST

NECK

ARMS

HANDS

STOMACH

GLUTES

THIGHS

CALVES

FEET

Notice any tension as you go. If you become aware of areas of gripping and tightness, breathe deeply into these places and intentionally release and relax your muscles.

MY BODY IS
WORTHY OF
RESPECT &
ACCEPTANCE

What do I wish I heard more from people?
How can I tell myself this and believe it?

_____
_____
_____
_____
_____
_____
_____
_____
_____
_____
_____
_____
_____
_____
_____

BRAIN DUMP

A Brain Dump is a great way to clear your mind of racing thoughts, ruminations and worries; figuratively 'dumping' all of your thoughts out onto paper. A clutter-free headspace will help you to feel less stressed, put things into perspective, and regain some focus and clarity.

You can pull this handy tool out whenever you need to, but you might find it particularly useful for times of anxiety or stress, or even for when your mind is so full of thoughts, ideas and creative inspiration that you just don't know where to start.

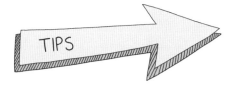

TIPS

✳ When doing a Brain Dump, try writing in a 'stream of consciousness' style, where you jot down each and every thought that pops into your mind, regardless of how big, small, 'relevant' or 'on-topic' it seems . . . You might be surprised what comes up.

✳ Your Brain Dump doesn't need to be neat and tidy or perfectly worded; you might like to use bullet points rather than full sentences, or even doodles and scribbles. Write down repeated thoughts or 'my mind is blank' thoughts, too!

HOW TO

STEP 1

Grab yourself some paper, a pen, and a comfy seat somewhere where you won't be distracted.

STEP 2

Set a timer for a length of time that doesn't feel too daunting — you might like to start with 5 minutes, even 1 minute is fine. If your brain is feeling super full right now, maybe you need 10 minutes or more.

STEP 3

Start the timer and 'get dumping'! Jot down each and every thought that comes to mind. Imagine the paper is now 'holding' these for you as you clear out more and more space in your head.

STEP 4

When you are finished you can either carry on with your day and new-found decluttered headspace, or perhaps you might like to look back over your Brain Dump (with compassion of course) and try out the exercise coming up, where we reflect back over your thoughts.

Use this space
to write out your
Brain Dump . . .

BRAIN DUMP REFLECTION

Let's look back over your Brain Dump and unpack some of the worries and thoughts you jotted down.

Have a read back over what you wrote.

How much of what you wrote down are worries or thoughts that are **within** your control to change or do something about?

How many of these thoughts are things that are **outside** of your control, pulling your focus and energy into a struggle that you have no power to do anything about (other than to change your thoughts about them and to shift your attention away from them)?

There are no right or wrong things to write, ways to do this, or ways to feel after this! Just use this tool as a way to declutter, reflect and gain insight.

Go back through each point on your Brain Dump and make a mark next to, or circle, all the things that are energy-sucking and out of your control.

· DINNER TONIGHT

· WEEKEND?

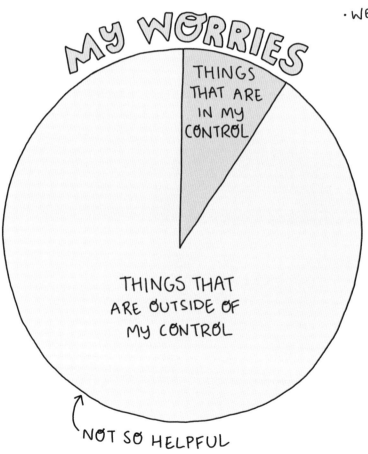

Reviewing your items again, how many of them are based in the past: ruminating or going over things that have already happened?

How many of them are in the future: worrying and stressing over things that are yet to take place (if they even do)?

And how many of them are based in the present moment: the here and now?

Go back through each point on your Brain Dump and make a mark to indicate if the thought is based in the past, present or future.

PAST   PRESENT   FUTURE

Write about a person who has had a great impact on your life.

_____

_____

_____

_____

_____

_____

_____

_____

_____

_____

_____

_____

_____

_____

_____

What times/settings are you most confident in?
What makes you feel this way?

_____

_____

_____

_____

_____

_____

_____

_____

_____

_____

_____

_____

_____

_____

_____

_____

NEXT STEP

Pick out 3 things from your Brain Dump that stand out to you the most; maybe they are your biggest worries right now, causing you the most stress and taking up the most room in your head. You're going to write them out and make a wee plan for what you can do about them.

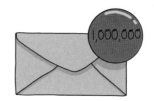

I have listed a couple of examples opposite to help get you started. Use the space below them to write your worries.

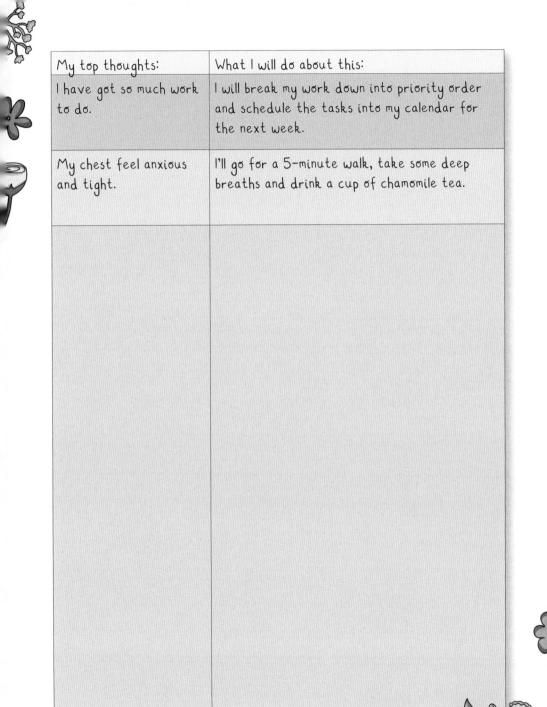

My top thoughts:	What I will do about this:
I have got so much work to do.	I will break my work down into priority order and schedule the tasks into my calendar for the next week.
My chest feel anxious and tight.	I'll go for a 5-minute walk, take some deep breaths and drink a cup of chamomile tea.

Write all the reasons why you are worthy of love and respect.

_____

_____

_____

_____

_____

_____

_____

_____

_____

_____

_____

_____

_____

_____

_____

_____

Thinking about the last week or two, when were you most happy?
What were you doing/thinking in these times?

_____

_____

_____

_____

_____

_____

_____

_____

_____

_____

_____

_____

_____

_____

_____

_____

_____

DAILY SELF CHECK-IN

Start your day by checking in with yourself. We never seem to take the time to stop and ask ourselves how we are and what we need. Now's your chance!

❋ How am I feeling right now?

❋ What thoughts am I having in this moment?

❋ How does my body physically feel today?

✳ What predictions am I making or assumptions do I have about my day ahead?

✳ Is anything from yesterday or this past week still impacting on me today? What do I need to do to release that today?

✳ What do I need to do today to support my wellbeing? (List a few simple things and a plan to action them.)

I am proud of myself for . . .

_____

_____

_____

_____

_____

_____

_____

_____

_____

_____

_____

_____

_____

_____

_____

_____

Think of a problem you are currently faced with. If this 'problem' could talk, what would it say it needs from you in order to be solved? What is it trying to teach you?

_____

_____

_____

_____

_____

_____

_____

_____

_____

_____

_____

_____

_____

_____

_____

_____

_____

_____

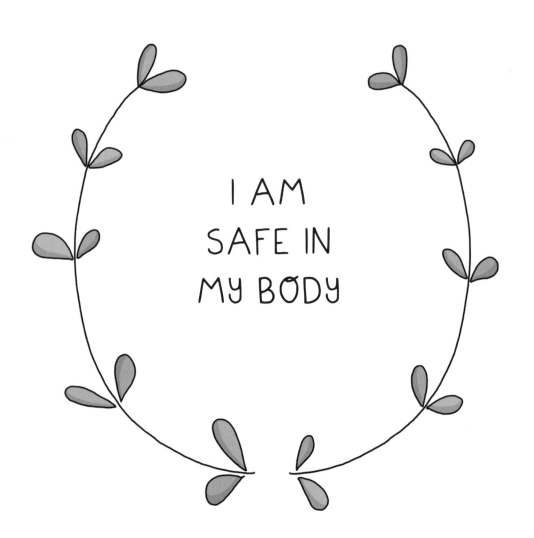

I AM
SAFE IN
MY BODY

What emotions do you want to feel more of in your life?
What are some things you can do to experience this?

_____

_____

_____

_____

_____

_____

_____

_____

_____

_____

_____

_____

_____

_____

_____

_____

MOOD TRACKER

Keeping track of your mood can help you to see the everyday fluctuations, gain perspective, and uncover any themes or triggers that may otherwise go undetected. When you feel anxious or down it is easy to think 'I always feel like this' and to slip into unhelpful thinking styles (more on these later).

In times like these it's hard to remember the good days. It's also easy to get 'swept away' with your emotions, following all your unhelpful thoughts down dark rabbit holes.

When you begin to track your mood, you put a bit of 'space' between you and 'the mood'. This space allows you to become more objective, to create distance between you and 'the feeling', to see that **you** are not **your emotions** and to **respond** rather than **react**.

This log will help you track and graph your mood over the next 2 weeks. It will give you a clearer and more accurate picture of how your mood changes day by day.

You are going to 'check in' with your emotions 3 times per day. A good way to do this is to set an alarm on your phone for 3 times throughout the day: morning, midday and evening. When the alarm goes off, take note of your mood and what is going on around you. (This will help you begin to identify if certain environments affect you or if there are certain things that are triggering different emotions, such as what you are thinking about at the time.)

Have a vague idea of a scale in your mind that works for **you**; e.g.

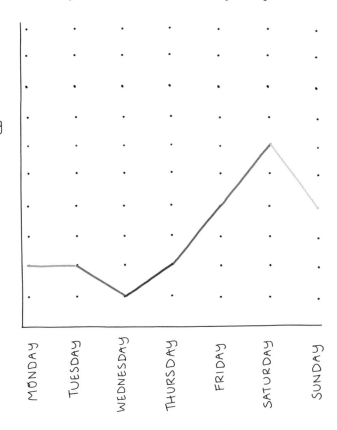

10/10 might be the best you have ever felt

7/10 might be feeling happy and relaxed

5/10 might be blah or just okay

2/10 might be really low or really anxious

0/10 might be the worst you have ever felt

MOOD

MONDAY TUESDAY WEDNESDAY THURSDAY FRIDAY SATURDAY SUNDAY

	8am check-in	12pm check-in	5pm check-in
Day 1	/10	/10	/10
Day 2	/10	/10	/10
Day 3	/10	/10	/10
Day 4	/10	/10	/10
Day 5	/10	/10	/10
Day 6	/10	/10	/10
Day 7	/10	/10	/10

Notes: (e.g. triggers, your thoughts or observations, the situations you were in)

You can graph your mood over the past week here:

MOOD

10

0

MONDAY TUESDAY WEDNESDAY THURSDAY FRIDAY SATURDAY SUNDAY

	8am check-in	12pm check-in	5pm check-in
Day 8	/10	/10	/10
Day 9	/10	/10	/10
Day 10	/10	/10	/10
Day 11	/10	/10	/10
Day 12	/10	/10	/10
Day 13	/10	/10	/10
Day 14	/10	/10	/10

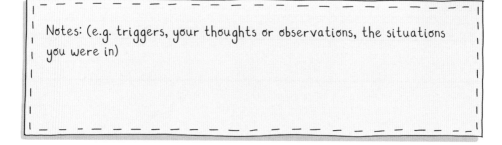

Notes: (e.g. triggers, your thoughts or observations, the situations you were in)

MOOD

10

0

MONDAY

TUESDAY

WEDNESDAY

THURSDAY

FRIDAY

SATURDAY

SUNDAY

Write about a difficult time in your life, how you got through it and what you learnt from this experience.

_____

_____

_____

_____

_____

_____

_____

_____

_____

_____

_____

_____

_____

_____

_____

_____

_____

_____

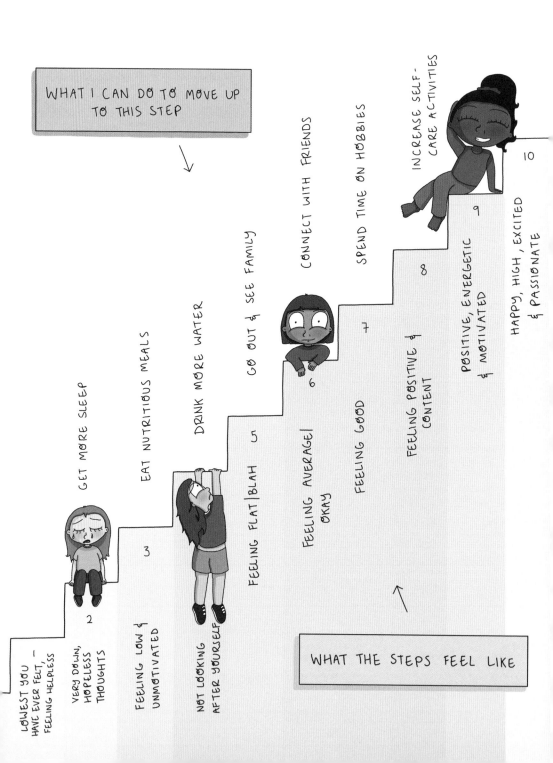

MOOD STAIRCASE

When you're feeling low it can feel overwhelming to know what steps you need to take to get back to a good place again. If you rate your mood at a 2/10, for example, getting yourself back to an 8/10 might feel like a mammoth or even impossible task!

A mood staircase is all about taking **one** step at a time to lift your mood. We can try small and manageable tasks to climb up and up until we are in a good place again.

ASK YOURSELF:

* What does a 2/10 look like for me?
  What am I doing/thinking/saying/not doing at a 2/10?

* What does an 8/10 look like for me?
  What am I doing/thinking/saying/not doing at an 8/10?

* What small steps could I take between each step that might boost my mood? What things have helped me in the past? (There are some examples in the illustration).

Create your OWN Mood Staircase — fill out the illustration on the following page with how you might be feeling at certain points on the staircase and a bunch of little things you could try out at different steps to lift your mood.

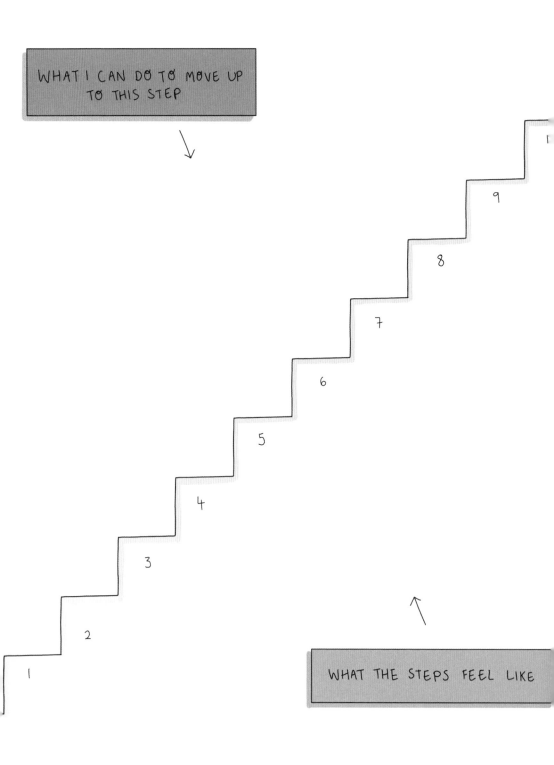

WHAT I CAN DO TO MOVE UP
TO THIS STEP

WHAT THE STEPS FEEL LIKE

1
2
3
4
5
6
7
8
9
1

GROWTH
MAY LOOK LIKE
STRUGGLE . . . .
UNTIL YOU EMERGE
OUT THE
OTHER SIDE

WARM FUZZIES LOG

	Today I am grateful for:	Today I achieved:	I am proud of myself for:	Someone I appreciate:
Day 1				
Day 2				
Day 3				
Day 4				
Day 5				
Day 6				
Day 7				

	Today I showed kindness when:	Today I witnessed kindness when:	A mantra I love today is:	My intention for tomorrow is:
Day 1				
Day 2				
Day 3				
Day 4				
Day 5				
Day 6				
Day 7				

Make a list of your goals and why they are important.

_____

_____

_____

_____

_____

_____

_____

_____

_____

_____

_____

_____

_____

_____

_____

_____

_____

_____

_____

What do you need to do in order to move towards your goals?

_____

_____

_____

_____

_____

_____

_____

_____

_____

_____

_____

_____

_____

_____

_____

_____

_____

_____

_____

FOUNDATIONS OF WELLBEING

It's easy to forget about the basics when it comes to your wellbeing. You might find yourself neglecting the simplest things, like drinking enough water, eating enough (healthy) food throughout the day, getting enough sleep and getting out and moving your body.

It's important to have your foundation in check before you can focus on higher needs and goals.

YOU DON'T START BUILDING A HOUSE IN THE ATTIC!

WORK ON BUILDING SOLID FOUNDATIONS...

...BEFORE MOVING ON TO HIGHER GOALS.

You can use these logs to set some goals and track your foundations of wellbeing over the next fortnight.

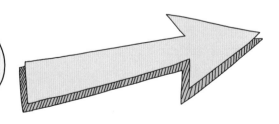

68

WATER INTAKE

Goal:

_____

glasses
per day

Day 1: _____
Day 2: _____
Day 3: _____
Day 4: _____
Day 5: _____
Day 6: _____
Day 7: _____

number of glasses per day

SLEEP

Goal:

_____

hours per night,
in bed by __pm,
up by __am

Day 1: _____
Day 2: _____
Day 3: _____
Day 4: _____
Day 5: _____
Day 6: _____
Day 7: _____

number of hours' sleep per night

EATING

GOOD
JOB

Goal:
Having __ meals and
__ snacks per day
and eating some more

_____

(name some types
of food)

Day 1: _____
Day 2: _____
Day 3: _____
Day 4: _____
Day 5: _____
Day 6: _____
Day 7: _____

tick if you met your nutritional goal

MOVEMENT

Goal:
Exercise/movement
of some form __ times
per week for __
minutes each
time

Day 1: _____
Day 2: _____
Day 3: _____
Day 4: _____
Day 5: _____
Day 6: _____
Day 7: _____

number of minutes of movement

WATER INTAKE

Goal:

_____

glasses
per day

Day 1: _____
Day 2: _____
Day 3: _____
Day 4: _____
Day 5: _____
Day 6: _____
Day 7: _____

number of glasses
per day

SLEEP

Goal:

_____

hours per night,
in bed by —pm,
up by —am

Day 1: _____
Day 2: _____
Day 3: _____
Day 4: _____
Day 5: _____
Day 6: _____
Day 7: _____

number of hours'
sleep per night

YOU GOT THIS

EATING

Goal:
Having — meals and
— snacks per day
and eating some more

_____

(name some types
of food)

Day 1: _____
Day 2: _____
Day 3: _____
Day 4: _____
Day 5: _____
Day 6: _____
Day 7: _____

tick if you met your
nutritional goal

MOVEMENT

Goal:
Exercise/movement
of some form — times
per week for —
minutes each
time

Day 1: _____
Day 2: _____
Day 3: _____
Day 4: _____
Day 5: _____
Day 6: _____
Day 7: _____

number of minutes
of movement

70

You can continue to track your foundations for a whole month right here:

Keep Going!

Day 1	Day 2	Day 3	Day 4	Day 5
WATER INTAKE:	WATER INTAKE:	WATER INTAKE:	WATER INTAKE:	WATER INTAKE:
____ glasses	____ glasses	____ glasses	____ glasses	____ glasses
SLEEP:	SLEEP:	SLEEP:	SLEEP:	SLEEP:
____ hours total	____ hours total	____ hours total	____ hours total	____ hours total
Did I eat well today? Y / N	Did I eat well today? Y / N	Did I eat well today? Y / N	Did I eat well today? Y / N	Did I eat well today? Y / N
MOVEMENT:	MOVEMENT:	MOVEMENT:	MOVEMENT:	MOVEMENT:
____ minutes	____ minutes	____ minutes	____ minutes	____ minutes
Day 6	Day 7	Day 8	Day 9	Day 10
WATER INTAKE:	WATER INTAKE:	WATER INTAKE:	WATER INTAKE:	WATER INTAKE:
____ glasses	____ glasses	____ glasses	____ glasses	____ glasses
SLEEP:	SLEEP:	SLEEP:	SLEEP:	SLEEP:
____ hours total	____ hours total	____ hours total	____ hours total	____ hours total
Did I eat well today? Y / N	Did I eat well today? Y / N	Did I eat well today? Y / N	Did I eat well today? Y / N	Did I eat well today? Y / N
MOVEMENT:	MOVEMENT:	MOVEMENT:	MOVEMENT:	MOVEMENT:
____ minutes	____ minutes	____ minutes	____ minutes	____ minutes

Day 11	Day 12	Day 13	Day 14	Day 15
WATER INTAKE: ___ glasses	WATER INTAKE: ___ glasses	WATER INTAKE: ___ glasses	WATER INTAKE: ___ glasses	WATER INTAKE: ___ glasses
SLEEP: ___ hours total	SLEEP: ___ hours total	SLEEP: ___ hours total	SLEEP: ___ hours total	SLEEP: ___ hours total
Did I eat well today? Y / N	Did I eat well today? Y / N	Did I eat well today? Y / N	Did I eat well today? Y / N	Did I eat well today? Y / N
MOVEMENT: ___ minutes	MOVEMENT: ___ minutes	MOVEMENT: ___ minutes	MOVEMENT: ___ minutes	MOVEMENT: ___ minutes
Day 16	Day 17	Day 18	Day 19	Day 20
WATER INTAKE: ___ glasses	WATER INTAKE: ___ glasses	WATER INTAKE: ___ glasses	WATER INTAKE: ___ glasses	WATER INTAKE: ___ glasses
SLEEP: ___ hours total	SLEEP: ___ hours total	SLEEP: ___ hours total	SLEEP: ___ hours total	SLEEP: ___ hours total
Did I eat well today? Y / N	Did I eat well today? Y / N	Did I eat well today? Y / N	Did I eat well today? Y / N	Did I eat well today? Y / N
MOVEMENT: ___ minutes	MOVEMENT: ___ minutes	MOVEMENT: ___ minutes	MOVEMENT: ___ minutes	MOVEMENT: ___ minutes

Day 21	Day 22	Day 23	Day 24	Day 25
WATER INTAKE:	WATER INTAKE:	WATER INTAKE:	WATER INTAKE:	WATER INTAKE:
____	____	____	____	____
glasses	glasses	glasses	glasses	glasses
SLEEP:	SLEEP:	SLEEP:	SLEEP:	SLEEP:
____	____	____	____	____
hours total	hours total	hours total	hours total	hours total
Did I eat well today? Y / N	Did I eat well today? Y / N	Did I eat well today? Y / N	Did I eat well today? Y / N	Did I eat well today? Y / N
MOVEMENT:	MOVEMENT:	MOVEMENT:	MOVEMENT:	MOVEMENT:
____	____	____	____	____
minutes	minutes	minutes	minutes	minutes
Day 26	Day 27	Day 28	Day 29	Day 30
WATER INTAKE:	WATER INTAKE:	WATER INTAKE:	WATER INTAKE:	WATER INTAKE:
____	____	____	____	____
glasses	glasses	glasses	glasses	glasses
SLEEP:	SLEEP:	SLEEP:	SLEEP:	SLEEP:
____	____	____	____	____
hours total	hours total	hours total	hours total	hours total
Did I eat well today? Y / N	Did I eat well today? Y / N	Did I eat well today? Y / N	Did I eat well today? Y / N	Did I eat well today? Y / N
MOVEMENT:	MOVEMENT:	MOVEMENT:	MOVEMENT:	MOVEMENT:
____	____	____	____	____
minutes	minutes	minutes	minutes	minutes

I DID IT!

What are some of your unhealthy habits that you are
going to work on cutting out? What healthy behaviours
or tools will you replace them with?

_____

_____

_____

_____

_____

_____

_____

_____

_____

_____

_____

_____

_____

_____

_____

_____

_____

_____

What are some new habits that will build your confidence and self-worth that you can weave into your life? How will you incorporate them, and how will you stick to them and hold yourself accountable?

_____

_____

_____

_____

_____

_____

_____

_____

_____

_____

_____

_____

_____

_____

_____

What activities, people and places in my life give me joy?

_____
_____
_____
_____
_____
_____
_____
_____
_____
_____
_____
_____
_____
_____
_____
_____
_____
_____

ALTERNATE NOSTRIL BREATHING

This breathing tool will help to lower your stress and anxiety levels, decrease your heart rate, help with headaches and improve your lung function.

STEP 1

Sit comfortably and exhale fully.

STEP 2

Bring your right hand to your face and use your right thumb to close your right nostril.

STEP 3

Inhale through your left nostril and then close your left nostril with your ring finger.

STEP 4

Exhale through your right nostril. Inhale through your right nostril and then close your right nostril with your thumb.

STEP 5

Exhale through your left nostril, then go back to step 3. Repeat.

Repeat this cycle for up to 5 minutes, finishing on an exhale.

What are 3 aspects of my personality
that I am proud of and love?

_____

_____

_____

_____

_____

_____

_____

_____

_____

_____

_____

_____

_____

_____

_____

WEIGHTED BREATH

This technique not only calms you down by slowing down your breath, it also provides proprioceptive input to the body — a super-grounding feeling of deep pressure that many of us respond really well to.

STEP 1

Lie down on the floor or your bed and grab a heavy blanket or something similar.

STEP 2

Place the blanket across your tummy and chest. You should feel a soothing amount of pressure and weight from the blanket.

STEP 3

Focus on your breath travelling down 'into your tummy'.

STEP 4

Try to make the blanket rise up and down with each inhale and exhale into your belly.

Breathe slowly and deeply for as long as you like, and take note of how calm and relaxed you feel at the end!

THE RESET BREATH

This tool is a great way to instantly relax your diaphragm and calm you down in times of stress!

STEP 1

Raise your arms and cross them above your head.

STEP 2

Take in the biggest breath you can.

STEP 3

Exhale as hard as you can out through your mouth.

Tip:
Only do this once or twice.

What are my 3 greatest strengths?
How do these shine in my life and how can I embrace them more?

_____

_____

_____

_____

_____

_____

_____

_____

_____

_____

_____

_____

_____

_____

_____

_____

_____

_____

What are my values? Do I feel my current behaviours are in line with these? What can I do to get more in line with my values?

_____

_____

_____

_____

_____

_____

_____

_____

_____

_____

_____

_____

_____

_____

_____

What does self-care mean to me? What barriers stop me prioritising self-care in my life? (thoughts, limiting beliefs, historical ideas about self-care)

_____

_____

_____

_____

_____

_____

_____

_____

_____

_____

_____

_____

_____

_____

_____

_____

_____

SCHEDULING SELF-CARE & FUN

Looking after yourself and having fun are crucial elements of wellbeing and happiness, so here is a JUMBO list of ideas to help you do just that... Tick or circle the things you are willing to try out, and then add some of your own in the spaces at the end.

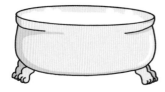

* Take a hot shower or bath
* Make a cup of tea
* Journal
* Tidy up an area of the house
* Call or text a friend

* Hang out with your pet
* Go for a walk
* Stand outside for some fresh air
* Listen to music

* Watch a funny TV series
* Watch a movie
* Play a board game
* Connect with family
* Meditate
* Do your favourite hobby
* Go swimming
* Go for a bike ride
* Dance
* Sing
* Draw
* Paint or do some art
* Make something
* Cook a meal

* Bake

* Paint your nails

* Get your washing done

* Sort your clothes

* Try an adventurous activity like hiking, sailing, surfing, etc.

* Enrol in an exercise class

* Go to the gym

* Do some yoga

* Do some stretching

* Cleanse your social media accounts

* Wash your hair

* Get a massage

* Do a face mask

* Try a guided audio meditation

* Go to the library

* Sit at a café and enjoy a hot drink

* Go to the beach, park, river . . .

* Go for a bike ride

* Read a book

* Watch funny YouTube videos

* Scroll through Pinterest for inspiration

* Invent a recipe

* Play an instrument

* Build something

* Practise mindfulness

* Take an online class

* Go shopping

* Plan a weekly menu

* Write out your goals

* Write a letter to a loved one

* Plan something with friends

* Go to dinner or the movies

Write your own ideas:

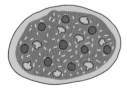

Use this calendar to schedule in an act of self-care or something fun each and every day for the next month. Don't get too hung up — it's okay to change out the item for something else on the day . . . or to do more than one!

Day 1	Day 2	Day 3	Day 4	Day 5
Day 6	Day 7	Day 8	Day 9	Day 10
Day 11	Day 12	Day 13	Day 14	Day 15

Day 16	Day 17	Day 18	Day 19	Day 20
Day 21	Day 22	Day 23	Day 24	Day 25
Day 26	Day 27	Day 28	Day 29	Day 30

How do I treat the people in my life that I love?
How can I treat myself this same way?

_____

_____

_____

_____

_____

_____

_____

_____

_____

_____

_____

_____

_____

_____

_____

What is 1 simple thing I can do today that will give me a boost?

_____
_____
_____
_____
_____
_____
_____
_____
_____
_____
_____
_____
_____
_____
_____
_____
_____

WORRY LIST

Write out a list
of your worries and
stressors here . . .

Pick out the top 3 worries on your list that are **outside** of your control	Something I can do to try to let go of this worry is . . .	A coping statement I can use when this worry pops up is . . .	A strategy I can use when this worry arises is . . .	Someone who can help me manage this worry is . . .
Worry 1:				
Worry 2:				
Worry 3:				

Pick out the top 3 worries on your list that are **within** your control	I will address this worry by . . . (write your plan of attack here)	I will do this by . . . (write the timeline in which you will get this sorted)	I will know I have sorted out my worry when . . .	Someone who can help me achieve this plan is . . .
Worry 1:				
Worry 2:				
Worry 3:				

I WILL HOLD MYSELF ACCOUNTABLE TO MY COMMITMENT TO ACCEPT AND LOVE MYSELF

Would you call yourself a worrier? Many people experience overthinking, frequent worrisome thoughts and anxious ruminations. These unhelpful thoughts often swirl around your head all day, causing you to feel stressed and panicky, and while you may waste a lot of your precious energy on these worries, you don't often actually achieve anything by doing so.

WORRY TIME

Some people have a belief (conscious or otherwise) that worrying about 'the thing' will somehow prevent 'the thing' from happening. As if ruminating on your worry will somehow prepare you to deal with it or keep it at bay. The truth is, worrying is a waste of energy and it achieves nothing at all. A more productive use of your time and energy is to take action on your worries, make plans and get proactive.

Worry Time is all about setting a particular time of the day when you do all of your worrying. Throughout the day, when your worries surface, gently tell them 'Not now, worry . . . You can come back at Worry Time', then you distract yourself and put the worry to the side.

This can be easier said than done, and breaking the 'worry habit' can take work! That's where this tool, Worry Time, can come in handy!

STEP
1

When your allocated Worry Time rolls around (e.g. 8pm), you sit down and you let yourself worry for 10 straight minutes (any more than this turns into a bit of an unproductive spiral). Now is the time to allow yourself to worry about all those things you pressed 'pause' on throughout your day.

STEP
2

At the end of your 10 minutes, you might like to pick a few of your biggest worries and make an action plan for addressing them, or write out some calming coping statements if they are out of your control to deal with.

STEP
3

When you have finished your Worry Time, it's back to pressing 'pause' on any worries that pop up until your Worry Time the next day.

PAUSE ❚❚

WORRY TIME PLAN:

My Worry
Time will be:

_____

(e.g. 8pm after dinner
and the kids are
in bed)

The statement I will use to press 'pause' on my worries:

(e.g. I see you, worry, but now is not the time.
I will hear you out at 8pm — come back later)

How I will stay distracted from the worry until Worry Time:

(e.g. I will go for a 2-minute walk and listen to music or
I will take 5 deep breaths and focus on what I should be doing)

Jot down your
'Worry Time worries'
as bullet points here:

Points for reflection: Did any worries
pop up over and over? Did it get
any easier to press 'pause' on your
worries throughout the week? Was
Worry Time a useful tool for you?

Pick a worry or two and make an action plan to address the worry here.

Worry:	Action plan:
I have too much work to do.	Break my workload down into tasks and manageable chunks, allot the time needed for each one, then schedule into my calendar for the next 2 weeks.
I'm going to make a fool of myself at the work social meeting this Friday night and no one will talk to me.	Use my coping statements, practise calming breathing exercises before I go in, find out if some people I know are going and make a plan to meet them there.

Is there something I am holding onto that evokes shame or regret for me? Write a letter to yourself here with words of compassion and forgiveness around this . . .

_____

_____

_____

_____

_____

_____

_____

_____

_____

_____

_____

_____

_____

_____

_____

_____

_____

_____

_____

If I loved myself, and nothing changed externally,
how would I treat myself differently?

_____

_____

_____

_____

_____

_____

_____

_____

_____

_____

_____

_____

_____

_____

_____

_____

_____

What are 5 things in my life I am grateful for?

_____

_____

_____

_____

_____

_____

_____

_____

_____

_____

_____

_____

_____

_____

_____

_____

_____

_____

UNHELPFUL THINKING STYLES

Most unhelpful thoughts tend to fall into
one of the following categories . . .

CATASTROPHISING

Blowing things out of
proportion

MIND READING

Assuming you know
what someone else is
thinking

FUTURE
PREDICTING

'What if's' and
making predictions
about what is going
to happen

FILTERING

Only focusing on
one part of
something, usually
the negative

SHOULD-ING

Being harsh or
demanding on yourself,
often saying
'I should . . .'

BLACK & WHITE

Seeing only one
extreme . . . good
or bad, right
or wrong

Often, unhelpful thoughts go unnoticed and unchallenged. We humans don't tend to do a lot of 'thinking about our thinking'! However, your thoughts play a major role in determining your emotions; the way you think influences the way you feel. When you notice you are feeling anxious, down or stressed, pay attention to your thoughts. Begin to notice the things you are telling yourself, the judgements you are making, the critical remarks about yourself and the fears that are bubbling away.

I'M NOTICING ANXIETY...
...TIME TO DO MY
THOUGHT LOG!

Once you start to notice these thoughts, you might just find they are unhelpful ones, like the examples opposite. And once you can recognise the thoughts for what they are:

  ✳ you realise that your thoughts do not have to control you.

  ✳ you understand that not all thoughts are helpful **or** true.

  ✳ you see that you can challenge your thoughts and create **new** more realistic and helpful ones.

  ✳ you choose to let go of your unhelpful thoughts, by not attaching judgement to them or wasting your energy on them.

UNHELPFUL THINKING LOG

Use this log over the next week to track your unhelpful thoughts. The easiest way to begin to spot them is to start working backwards from an event or situation that triggered off a strong emotion for you. When you notice that feeling of anxiety, stress or sadness, this is your cue to dive a little deeper and fill out this log!

What happened? (what was the situation, where were you, who were you with, etc.)	How were you feeling?	What were you thinking? (what thoughts, images, fears, predictions, etc., came to mind)	What did you do/ how did you act because of these thoughts/feelings?
e.g. At the end of a staff meeting, my boss said he needed to speak with me privately in his office.	Anxious, panicking, scared, embarrassed.	'I'm in trouble.' 'He's going to tell me off and I can't cope.' 'Everyone in the meeting will be scoffing at me behind my back.' 'What if I get fired?'	Talked about him behind his back to a staff member. Went home sick.

What happened? (what was the situation, where were you, who were you with, etc.)	How were you feeling?	What were you thinking? (what thoughts, images, fears, predictions, etc., came to mind)	What did you do/ how did you act because of these thoughts/feelings?

Are there areas in my life where I hold a 'victim mindset'?
What can I do to shift out of this and into my power?

_____
_____
_____
_____
_____
_____
_____
_____
_____
_____
_____
_____
_____
_____
_____
_____
_____

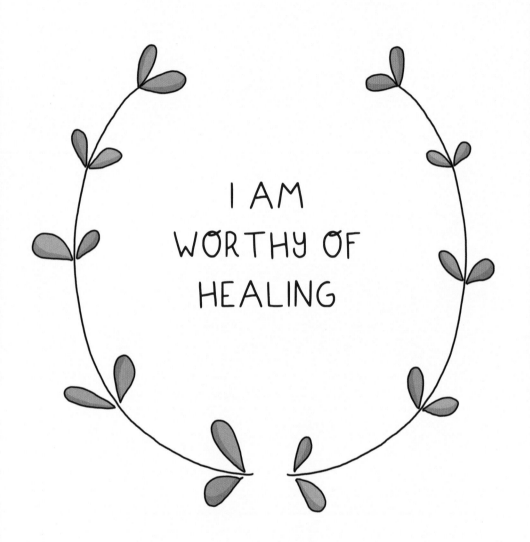

I AM
WORTHY OF
HEALING

What 'coping strategies' were modelled to me as a child?
How do these play out in my life now?

_____
_____
_____
_____
_____
_____
_____
_____
_____
_____
_____
_____
_____
_____
_____
_____
_____

CHALLENGING YOUR UNHELPFUL THOUGHTS

Here are some questions you can ask yourself to help you **challenge** those pesky unhelpful thoughts. In doing this, you will be able to 're-write' the thought, replacing it with a coping statement or a new, more balanced and rational thought, **based in fact**.

* Is this an unhelpful thought? What type of thinking style could this be?

* Am I confusing this thought with a fact or jumping to conclusions?

* What evidence do I have that does **not** support this thought?

* If my friend had this thought, what would I say to them?

* Do I know for sure this thought is true? If not, why not?

* What is a more likely/true thought?

* What else could be true?

* Am I taking something too personally?

* What is the worst thing that could realistically happen, and what could I do to cope if it did?

* Am I asking myself questions with no answers?

* Am I focusing on my weak points and ignoring my strengths?

* Am I overestimating the threat here?

* Am I assuming I have zero control over this?

* Is this a double standard? (Would I say this to a loved one?)

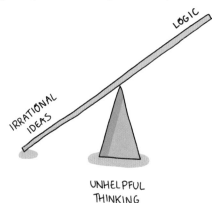

LOGIC

IRRATIONAL IDEAS

UNHELPFUL THINKING

FEARS

LOGIC, REALITY & FACTS

BALANCED THINKING

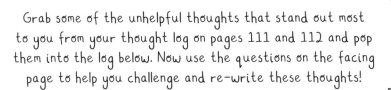

Grab some of the unhelpful thoughts that stand out most to you from your thought log on pages 111 and 112 and pop them into the log below. Now use the questions on the facing page to help you challenge and re-write these thoughts!

My unhelpful thought:	A more helpful thought:
e.g. 'I'm in trouble'	'He could want to speak with me about anything. It's unlikely I'm in trouble, but if I am I will deal with it and rectify the problem.'
'What if I get fired?'	'I can't be fired, as I haven't had any warnings. I am good at my job. This is more likely to be a completely non-threatening conversation.'

My unhelpful thought:	A more helpful thought:

You can use these logs to continue unpacking your unhelpful thoughts . . .

Situation or trigger (What happened? Where? With who? When? How?)	Emotions (How did you feel? What did you notice in your body?)	Unhelpful thoughts (What thoughts or images were in your mind?)

Actions (How did you act/behave when this happened?)	Unhelpful thinking style (e.g. catastrophising, future predicting)	More helpful thoughts (Challenge your thoughts and write some more realistic ones here)

Situation or trigger (What happened? Where? With who? When? How?)	Emotions (How did you feel? What did you notice in your body?)	Unhelpful thoughts (What thoughts or images were in your mind?)

Actions (How did you act/behave when this happened?)	Unhelpful thinking style (e.g. catastrophising, future predicting)	More helpful thoughts (Challenge your thoughts and write some more realistic ones here)

TIME FOR ANOTHER BRAIN DUMP!

Remember the Brain Dump you did back on page 35? Well, it's time for another one! If you've forgotten how, flick back and re-read the instructions.

Once you have done this in the space opposite, go back to your first Brain Dump on page 35 and read this again. Are there any thoughts that are **'repeat thoughts'** — ones that appear on both Brain Dumps? If so, write them in the log on page 124 and make a plan to either tackle the worry or come up with a compassionate 'coping statement' to help you better face this thought if it keeps popping up in the future.

Let's get started!
Use this space to write
out your Brain Dump . . .

Here's a couple of examples to get you started:

My repeat (or top 3) thoughts:	What I will do about this:
I have a million emails to get to.	I will set aside 15 minutes each morning for the next week to go through them, deleting and replying as I go.
I'm so unhappy with my body right now.	I will start practising gratitude statements for the functions my body performs. I'll do them in the shower each night for 5 minutes. Coping statement to use when I think this thought during the day: 'I am enough just as I am. I don't need to compare myself to anyone.'

If there are no repeat thoughts, then you can just pick the top 3 that stand out for you, like you did in the first Brain Dump.

REPEAT

What boundaries do I need to set with myself?

_____

_____

_____

_____

_____

_____

_____

_____

What boundaries do I need to set with others?

_____

_____

_____

_____

_____

_____

_____

_____

When I love myself, what are some things I do each day to show this?

_____

_____

_____

_____

_____

_____

_____

_____

_____

_____

_____

_____

_____

_____

_____

_____

_____

_____

WORRY DIARY

Pick a worry you are troubled by at the moment.

What is your worry or
unhelpful thought?

Rate how much you
believe the worry:

```
0              5             10
|--------------|--------------|
Don't       It could be     Totally
believe it     true        convinced
                          it is true
```

e.g. catastrophising, future
predicting, etc.

What type of unhelpful
thinking style could this be?

Realistically, how likely
is it that the worry
will happen?

Colour
here

0%.   100%.

What is more likely to happen?

128

Is this worry out of my control? Yes ☐ No ☐

Could I do anything to problem-solve or ease this worry? Yes ☐ No ☐

What are some more balanced/helpful/realistic thoughts?

If my worry did happen, what could I do about it and who could help?

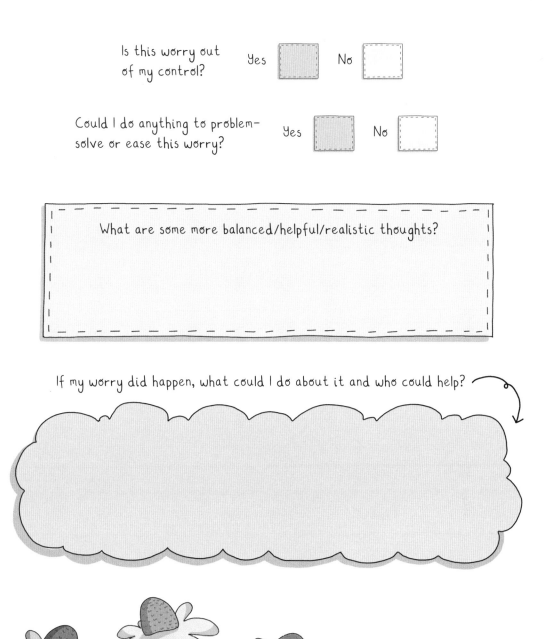

MY VOICE
AND NEEDS
MATTER

Make a list of situations that make you anxious or uncomfortable. Write about ways you can shift your mindset and actions to face these fears and get more comfortable in these settings.

_____

_____

_____

_____

_____

_____

_____

_____

_____

_____

_____

_____

_____

_____

_____

_____

_____

_____

_____

MY UNHELPFUL THOUGHTS CHEAT SHEET

When your thoughts are spiralling and getting on top of you, it's normal to keep circling back to the same old ruminations and unhealthy beliefs about yourself. During these times it is tricky to 'push back' against your thoughts and challenge them.

That's where this cheat sheet comes in. Pre-empt the spiral and get ahead of the game by jotting down a list of the thoughts that trip you up the most, and then some healthy coping statements and more realistic thoughts right there next to them. Next time you feel yourself sinking back into those old patterns and unhelpful narratives, grab this journal and flick straight to this page!

Write out some of the most common unhelpful thoughts, worries and negative beliefs that you have about yourself here, and then create a list of kick-ass rebuttals right next-door . . .

MY CHEAT SHEET

Here are a few examples to get you started:

When I think . . . (my Spiral thoughts)	I will tell myself . . . (my Healthy thoughts)
I'm not good enough.	I am worthy just as I am. I am more than enough.
I'm ugly.	My worth is NOT determined by the way I look. I am grateful to my body for all the functions it performs for me every day.
I can't cope. I can't do this.	I have got through hard times before and I will do it again. I am stronger than I give myself credit for.

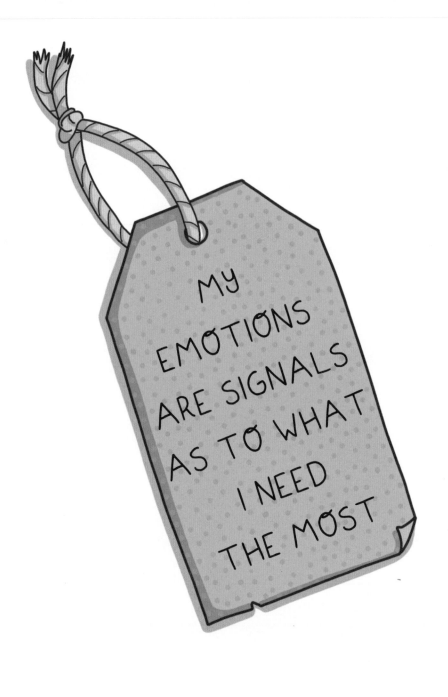

What makes me feel alive and passionate?

_____
_____
_____
_____
_____
_____
_____
_____
_____
_____
_____
_____
_____
_____
_____
_____
_____
_____
_____
_____
_____

So many of us don't feel comfortable in our own skin. Does any of this sound like you . . . ?

🌸 You pick out and feel overly aware of all your flaws.

🌸 You are overly critical of yourself every time you look in the mirror.

🌸 You make harsh comments on your size and appearance to yourself and in conversation.

🌸 When a group or family photo is taken and you're in it, you look straight to yourself to see how you are looking, rather than think how nice it is that you are all together.

🌸 You compare yourself to others.

🌸 You get caught on an image as you are scrolling through social media and fixate on all the reasons that person looks better than you, then feel bad about yourself.

How would you describe yourself? (Write about physical appearance, your personality, how you act around people, your social skills, your 'social status', your education, your strengths and weaknesses, your lifestyle . . .)

Go back and read over your self-description — pick out any harsh comments, negative self-judgements, labels you place on yourself and any pejorative language (words that are critical, harsh, of low opinion or show a lack of respect for self). Write these comments opposite and then take some time to re-write them in either a factual or more compassionate way. See some examples below.

Unhelpful description	New description
I'm lanky.	I'm 5'11. (factual)
I'm awkward around new people.	I like to get to know people before I open up and show my true self. (more compassionate)
My face is covered in pimples.	I experience some hormonal acne around my chin related to my cycle. (factual)
I'm a loner.	I really enjoy my own company. (compassionate)

DISTORTED|HARSH
VIEW OF SELF

REALISTIC|NON-EXAGGERATED
VIEW OF SELF

Unhelpful description	New description

You'll notice that your new descriptions still include the parts of yourself that you might be critical of. When you work towards boosting your self-worth and creating more self-confidence, you don't have to use overly positive statements that don't feel true or believable to you. We aren't here to create fantasy statements and throw glitter at everything! Our goal is to be **factual** and to be **compassionate**.

Now, re-write your self-description, replacing any of the harsh statements and pejorative language with your **new** descriptions. If you feel up for it, try to add in even **more** positive qualities, strengths and compassionate statements. How would your best friend describe you . . . ?

_____

_____

_____

_____

_____

_____

_____

_____

_____

_____

_____

Go back and re-read your new description. How does this feel compared to your first one?

Write a page full of statements of gratitude (for yourself, your body, your life), statements of self-acceptance, love and compassion, and a list of all your best qualities. Think of all your positive traits and every compliment you have ever received.

* I am a great friend.

* I am grateful to my body for the things it does for me.

* I deserve to treat my body with respect — I only get one!

* I love how open and honest I am. I'm also loyal and loving.

* I'm working on being kinder in the way I talk to myself.

* I'm good at being organised and I'm working on knowing that I don't have to do everything perfectly to be worthy or accepted.

_____

_____

_____

_____

_____

_____

_____

_____

Write a love letter to yourself
(there is no right or wrong way to do this!)

_____

_____

_____

_____

_____

_____

_____

_____

_____

_____

_____

_____

_____

_____

_____

_____

_____

I AM WORTHY
OF A BEAUTIFUL
LIFE

If I woke up tomorrow and a miracle had happened overnight while I slept, and when I opened my eyes my 'problem' was gone . . . What would happen differently in my day? What are some of the first things I would notice that would tell me things had changed?

_____

_____

_____

_____

_____

_____

_____

_____

_____

_____

_____

_____

_____

_____

CELEBRATING YOUR STRENGTHS

Humans have a tendency to something called a 'negativity bias': we are more prone to noticing our failures and weak points and the negative aspects of our lives. This trait is actually an evolutionary survival mechanism! It made sense in our caveman days to be on the look-out for threats, as they were real and ever-present. It also made sense to be aware of our flaws and shortcomings, so we could take steps to rectify these to better 'fit in' with our tribe. And it was crucial that we fit in for protection! These days, however, this 'negativity bias' is a feature that tends to make us more vulnerable to depression and to low self-esteem.

The good news is we can sway this bias in favour of a more positive outlook by seeking out our strengths and by practising gratitude. Over the next week, fill out this log with the prompts provided and experiment with recognising the 'wins' in your life.

MON DAY

A strength I have is . . . _____

and I noticed this today when . . . _____

_____

_____

TUES DAY

3 things I am thankful for today . . .

✳ _____

✳ _____

✳ _____

WEDNES DAY

Something I really loved about today was . . . _____

_____

_____

I am proud of myself for . . . _____

_____

_____

THURS DAY

Today I am so thankful for (person's name here) _____

_____ because _____

_____

_____

FRI DAY

Looking back on the week, the highlights have been . . .

_____

_____

Something I have learnt is . . . _____

_____

_____

SATUR DAY

This weekend I want to focus on . . . _____

_____

_____

I plan to be kind to myself by . . . _____

_____

SUN DAY

My intention for the week ahead is . . . _____

_____

_____

Some things I will do to look after myself are . . . _____

_____

What are my weaknesses? How can I work on these?

_____
_____
_____
_____
_____
_____
_____
_____
_____
_____
_____
_____
_____
_____
_____
_____
_____
_____

What are my strengths? How can I use these more in my life?

_____

_____

_____

_____

_____

_____

_____

_____

_____

_____

_____

_____

_____

_____

_____

_____

_____

_____

BODY GRATITUDE

Imagine how different your life could be if, instead of focusing on your flaws and being critical of your body, you celebrated yourself. Picture what it would be like to have a healthy and positive relationship with your body. One where you felt gratitude towards it for the functions it performs, rather than directing harsh and critical comments towards yourself each time you steal a glimpse of your reflection in the mirror. You are going to begin the work towards this shift in perception right now. This is a month-long log for you to fill in, noting something, no matter how small, about your body each day that shows either gratitude, forgiveness, acceptance, compassion or straight LOVE!

I am thankful to my eyes for allowing me to see my family

I love my arms

I am sorry to my tummy for the harsh words I have thought

Day 1	Day 2	Day 3	Day 4	Day 5
Day 6	Day 7	Day 8	Day 9	Day 10

Day 11	Day 12	Day 13	Day 14	Day 15
Day 16	Day 17	Day 18	Day 19	Day 20
Day 21	Day 22	Day 23	Day 24	Day 25
Day 26	Day 27	Day 28	Day 29	Day 30

What would a perfect day look like for me?

_____

_____

_____

_____

_____

_____

_____

_____

_____

_____

_____

_____

_____

_____

_____

_____

_____

NOT-SO-SECRET ADMIRER

Think about someone in your life who you love and admire.

Use this space to write down a list of all the qualities about that person that you value and are grateful for. What is it about them that makes them so special?

_____

_____

_____

_____

_____

_____

_____

_____

_____

_____

Just a thought . . . You might like to share the love and show them this list!

Go back over your list of lovely qualities and ask yourself this: What do all of these traits have in common?

_____

_____

_____

Here's my bet . . . They are **all internal characteristics** . . . The things that we admire and love about people are almost always entirely based on aspects that are within them. We don't care about the way they look, their social or financial status, their job, their house or their car . . . We value all of the personal traits that live **inside their soul**. Despite this . . . How often do you judge yourself based on external factors?! The truth is . . . These external things are not what others value about you, nor are they the things that make you a worthy or loveable person.

Have a look over the list of traits you admire about your loved one and pick the 3 things that stand out to you the most. Write them here:

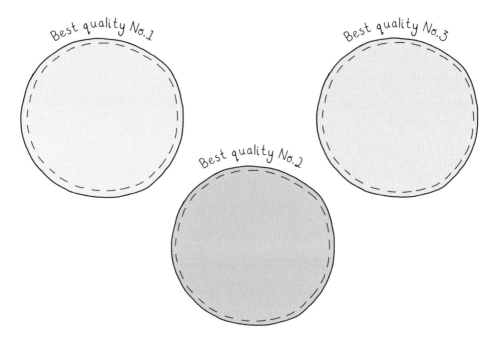

Let's turn the spotlight on you and your fabulous self now! Take this space to write about how **YOU** embody those top 3 qualities that you admire and value so much in your loved one.

Think up as many examples as you can for each quality — go ahead and give yourself a well-deserved ego-boost! If you get stuck, you could chat to a friend about this activity and get them to help you see that you **do**, in fact, have these wonderful qualities (and more) inside of yourself.

I am _____

and I know this because . . . _____

_____

_____

I am _____

and I know this because . . . _____

_____

_____

I am _____

and I know this because . . . _____

_____

_____

_____

I LOOK FOR
MOMENTS TO BE
GRATEFUL FOR
IN MY LIFE

Anxiety is a normal human emotion. Remind yourself that it will pass and you are safe.

 Breathe! Take time each day to check in with your breath. Take long, slow breaths deep down into your belly.

 Calm and soothe your body and mind with a cup of chamomile tea.

 Distraction can be a useful tool to shift your focus away from unhelpful thoughts and behaviours.

 Eat a balanced diet rich in antioxidants and exercise often.

 Friends and family. Surround yourself with support, and prioritise healthy connections and relationships.

 Ground yourself in the present moment by tuning into your senses, your body and your breath.

 Healthy habits. Create positive daily rituals of self-care.

 Inner critic. Get to know yours, and learn to keep it in check with self-compassion.

 Journal. Write out your feelings, thoughts, fears, goals and dreams to help you process them.

 Keep clear boundaries for yourself and others. It's okay to say no.

 Laugh. Find time for fun. Let your hair down. Keep it light and find the humour in life.

 Mindfulness. Observe your thoughts and emotions without judgement. Be present.

Name your emotions. Acknowledge them without judgement. Allow them to be.

Obstacles provide you a chance to look for opportunities and options for growth.

Plan and prioritise. Keep lists of schedules and don't overload yourself. Book in down-time and self-care.

Quiet. Give your mind and senses a break. Turn off and tune out.

Rest! It's okay to do nothing sometimes. Put your feet up, grab a cuppa and read a book or take a nap.

Sleep. It's so important to get enough sleep each night. Prioritise a soothing wind-down routine before bed.

Technology-free time. Spend time each day away from your screens, especially before bed.

Unique. You are the best at being you. Try not to compare yourself with others.

Values. Try to align your actions with what matters the most to you.

Water. Make sure you are drinking enough water each day — and not just in your coffee!

eXamine your unhelpful thoughts and challenge them. Remember, not all thoughts are true!

Yoga. Tune in, notice where you feel tension. Move your body. Honour this mind-body connection.

Zero tolerance for things in your life that don't honour your worthiness.

First published in 2021

Copyright©Rebekah Ballagh 2021

Allen & Unwin
Level 2, 10 College Hill
Auckland 1011, New Zealand
Phone: (64 9) 377 3800

Email: info@allenandunwin.com
Web: www.allenandunwin.co.nz

83 Alexander Street
Crows Nest NSW 2065, Australia
Phone: (61 2) 8425 0100

A catalogue record for this book is available
from the National Library of New Zealand

ISBN 978 1 98854 791 6

Design by Kate Barraclough
Printed and bound in China by C & C Printing Co., Ltd.

10 9 8 7 6 5 4 3 2 1

MIX
Paper from
responsible sources
FSC® C008047
FSC
www.fsc.org